Krisann Nething

Lifestyle of Liberty Workbook
Published by Lifestyle of Liberty Ministry
Houston, Texas
www.lifestyleoflibertyministry.org

Copyright © 2016 by Krisann Nething
ISBN: 978-0---9972407-0-2

All rights reserved. No part of this book may be reproduced without written permission from the publisher or copyright holder, except in the case of brief quotations embodied in critical articles and reviews. No part of this book may be transmitted in any form or by any means—electronic, mechanical, photocopy, recording, or other—without prior written permission from the publisher or copyright holder.

Scripture quotations are from the Holy Bible, New International Version® NIV® Copyright © 1973, 1978, 1984, 2011 by Biblica, Inc.TM Used by permission of Zondervan. All rights reserved worldwide. www.zondervan.com The "NIV" and "New International Version" are trademarks registered in the United States Patent and Trademark Office by Biblica, Inc.TM
Scripture quotations are from the Amplified® Bible, copyright © 1954, 1958, 1962, 1964, 1965, 1987 by The Lockman Foundation. Used by permission.(www.Lockman.org)
Ladder clipart from korobovaoksana © 123RF.com
Clipart of trees and Bible from 123RF.com

For more information go to www.lifestyleoflibertyministry.org
Or email lifestyleoflibertyKN@gmail.com

Krisann's heart's desire is to honor the many ministries that have impacted her over the years including Exchanged Life, Restoring the Foundations and Encounter God, by combining invaluable material from each along with over twenty-five years of ministry and personal experience, drawing the rich ministry into one study to further set captives free. Her prayer is for God to bless this and take it where He can. This is her part in the big picture of what God is doing in bringing freedom to His children.

Krisann would like to dedicate this work to:
Gary Nething, her husband and best friend, who she admires exceedingly. He is her #1 fan and encourager. She so appreciates and enjoys his partnership in life and ministry.
Gabi Soltau, always a faithful friend, the catalyst who prompted the creation of LOL.
Pastor Fernando Ruata, who has been a support to Krisann personally and to the vision of LOL, giving it a platform in the church.
Wendy Keen, who took Krisann's handouts and in union with the Holy Spirit, transformed them in to the first workbook.
Chester and Betsy Kylstra who gave permission for her to draw extensively from their fabulous work.

Krisann and her family were missionaries to Spain for 10 years and currently attend Encourager Church where she and Gary have been serving for many years in the Healing Rooms and Restoring the Foundations Ministry. Krisann and her husband have three grown children.

It truly is for freedom Christ has set us free.
God bless you on your journey as you are
transformed from one degree of glory to the next.
I am praying for you!

-Krisann

Not expecting perfection from myself or others frees grace.

Not looking toward when things will get better frees gratitude.

Understanding that we should not expect the road here to be Free from bumps fuels contentment and opens my heart to the Presence of God.

Table of Contents

Week One
Foundation for Change...1

Week Two
Power for Victory..9

Week Three
Understanding our Struggle..19
Activation: Open Doors of Occult, Infirmities, Idolatry, Rebellion, Addictions, Escape, Financial Problems, Mocking, Not Motivated

Week Four
Repentance/Forgiveness..27
"Real" Thoughts on Perfection & Pride
Activation: Open Doors of Performance, Shame, Bound Emotions, Unworthiness, Depression, Emotional Dependency, Failure, Pride, Religion

Week Five
Vows/Judgments..37
"Real" Thoughts on Abandonment & Rejection
Activation: Open Doors of Abandonment, Neglect, Orphan Lifestyle, Rejection, Victimization, Anxiety, Death, Identity Issues, Fear

Week Six
Soul Ties..47
"Real" Thoughts on Anger
Activation: Open Doors of Anger, Bitterness, Deception, Grief, Mental Problems, Trauma, Unbelief, Violence, Control, Sexual Bondage

Week Seven
Renewing the Mind...55
"Real" Thoughts on Rebellion
Activation: Renewing the Mind

Week Eight
The Shame, Fear, Control Connection...69
"Real" Thoughts on Fear and Unbelief
Activation: Renewing the Mind

Week Nine
Healing Wounds/Memories of the Past...77
Activation: Wounds of the Past

Week Ten
Defeating Our Enemy...85
Activation: Cast Out, All open doors

Week Eleven
Week of Modeling..91
Activation: Wounds of the Past

Week Twelve
Keys to Walking in Victory..97

Prayers..101

Open Doors...109

Endnotes..117

Week One

Foundation for Change

Week 1 — Foundation for Change

A Look at our Choices
This Is the Summary and the Message

Galatians 5:16 So I say, Live (walk) by the Spirit, and you will not gratify (fulfill) the desires of the flesh (sinful nature).

> **What happened when I got saved?**

First let's answer the question, *Why did I need to get saved?*

- **2 Problems:**
  - Our sin
  - Our spirit (which was dead)

The Sin Problem: Our Choices

Isaiah 59:2 But your iniquities have separated you from your God; your sins have hidden his face from you, so that He will not hear.

- **2 Trees Representing our Choices:**
  - Self life versus eternal life
  - Flesh is all I am apart from Christ

The Problem of Our Dead Spirit

- **Ephesians 2:1** As for you, you were dead in your transgressions and sins...
- **Identity**
- **Way of relating to God**

The Source of My Flesh

- What is our flesh and where does it come from?
- Man as a three part being: body, soul, spirit

1 Thessalonians 5:23 May God Himself, the God of peace, sanctify you through and through. May your whole spirit, soul and body be kept blameless at the coming of our Lord Jesus Christ.

Two Keys to Victory

*The Lordship of Jesus
*The Love of God

Foundation for Change

God's Solution

2 Corinthians 5:21 God made him who had no sin to be sin for us, so that in Him we might become the righteousness of God.

Colossians 2:13 When you were dead in your sins and in the uncircumcision of your flesh, God made you alive with Christ. He forgave us all our sins.

Notes:

_____

_____

_____

_____

_____

_____

_____

_____

_____

_____

_____

_____

_____

_____

LIVE BY THE SPIRIT
AND YOU WILL NOT GRATIFY THE DESIRES OF THE FLESH
Galatians 5:16

FLESH	SPIRIT
DISOBEDIENCE	OBEDIENCE
INDEPENDENCE	DEPENDENCE
BONDAGE	FREEDOM
LAW	GRACE
FACT	TRUTH
RULES	RELATIONSHIP
DEATH	LIFE

Flesh is all that I am apart from Christ

_____
_____
_____

STRIVE	**ABIDE**
DO	BE
COMPETE	Prefer/Encourage
FEAR	**TRUST**

PERSON BEFORE CHRIST

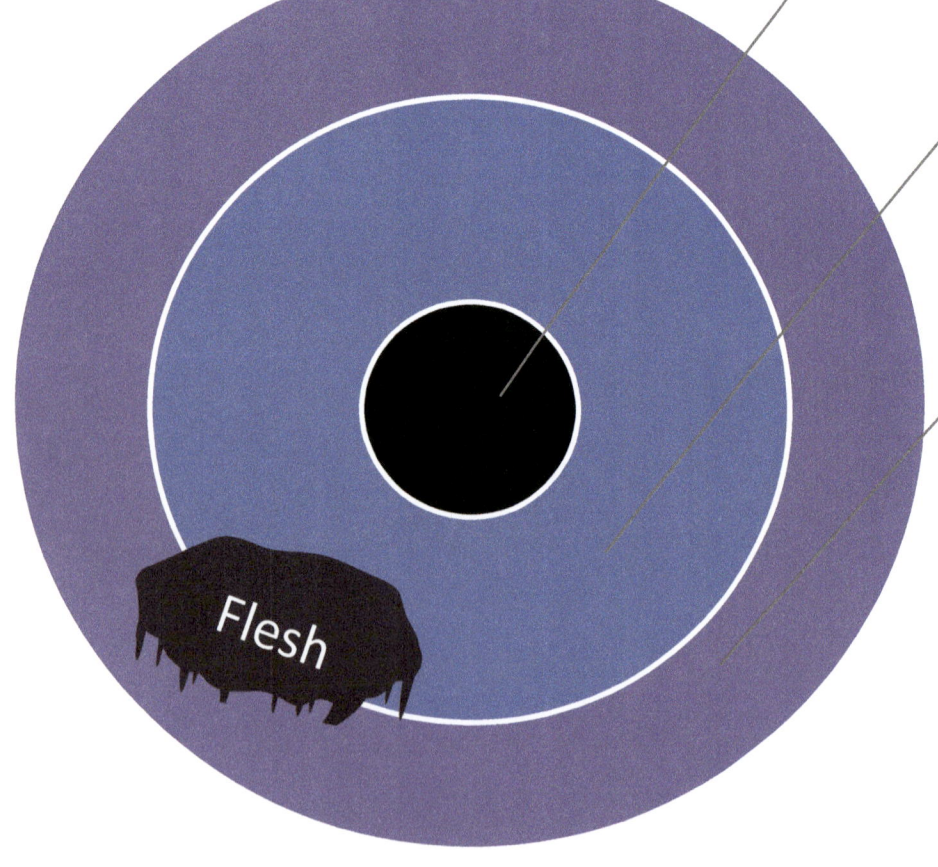

PERSON AFTER SALVATION

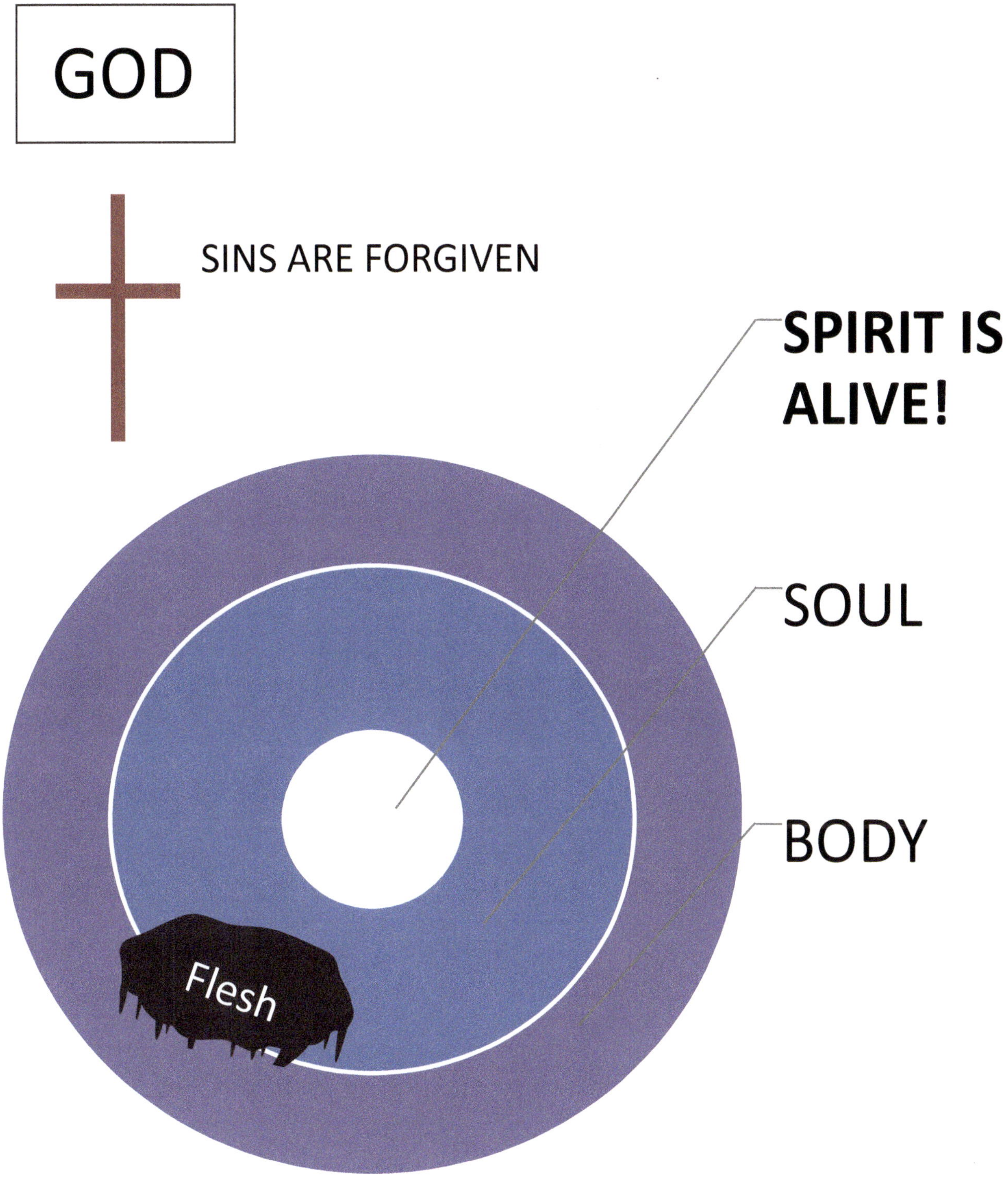

GOD

SINS ARE FORGIVEN

SPIRIT IS ALIVE!

SOUL

BODY

Flesh

Week Two

Power for Victory

Week 2 — Power for Victory

A Look at Adam and Eternal Life

Adam

1 Corinthians 15:21-22 For since [it was] through a man that death [came into the world, it is] also through a Man that the resurrection of the dead [has come]. For just as [because of their union of nature] in Adam all people die, so also [by virtue of their union of nature] shall all in Christ be made alive.

Romans 5:12-19 SINNED: Therefore, just as sin entered the world through one man, and death through sin, and in this way death came to all people, because all sinned—DIED (spiritually), For if the many died by the trespass of the one man, WERE CONDEMNED -the judgment followed one sin and brought condemnation; one trespass resulted in condemnation for all people, WERE MADE SINNERS- Through the disobedience of the one man the many were made sinners.

(Wording redacted from this verse - explanation added & not exact quotation)

Eternal Life

1John 1:2 The life appeared; we have seen it and testify to it, and we proclaim to you the eternal life, which was with the Father and has appeared to us.

1John 5:12 He who has the Son has life.

1John 5:20 He is the true God and eternal life. (Zoe)

Christ's *Timeline:* eternity past, birth, death, resurrection and eternity future

Colossians 1:16 For in Him all things were created… all things have been created through Him and for Him.

Philippians 2:7 rather, He made Himself nothing by taking the very nature of a servant, being made in human likeness…

John 1:14 The Word became flesh and made His dwelling among us.

Romans 5:8 But God demonstrates His own love for us in this: While we were still sinners, Christ died for us.

Ephesians 1:20 …. when He raised Christ from the dead and seated Him at his right hand in the heavenly realms…

Philippians 2:9 Therefore God exalted Him to the highest place and gave Him the name that is above every name…

Power for Victory

Eternal Life (cont.)

Our *Timeline* in Christ

Ephesians 1:4 For He chose us in Him before the creation of the world...

Galatians 2:20 I have been crucified with Christ...

Romans 6:4-5 We were therefore buried with Him through baptism into death in order that, just as Christ was raised from the dead through the glory of the Father, we too may live a new life. For if we have been united with Him in a death like His, we will certainly also be united with Him in a resurrection like His.

Ephesians 2:6 And God raised us up with Christ and seated us with Him in the heavenly realms in Christ Jesus...

Colossians 3:4 When Christ, who is your life, appears, then you also will appear with Him in glory.

Eternal life is Christ's life!

What Happens at Salvation
A Look at The Transfer and Being Born Again

The Transfer

Colossians 2:13 When you were dead in your sins and in the uncircumcision of your flesh, God made you alive with Christ. He forgave us all our sins.

Colossians 1:13-14 For He has rescued us from the dominion of darkness and brought (to transfer, that is, carry away, depose or (figuratively) exchange) us into the kingdom of the Son He loves, in whom we have redemption, the forgiveness of sins.

Ephesians 2:4-5 But because of His great love for us, God, who is rich in mercy, made us alive with Christ even when we were dead in transgressions--it is by grace you have been saved.

I Peter 3:18 For Christ also suffered once for sins, the righteous for the unrighteous, to bring you to God...

Power for Victory

Born Again

1 Peter 1:23 For you have been born again, not of perishable seed, but of imperishable, through the living and enduring word of God.

Galatians 3:16 The promises were spoken to Abraham and to his seed. Scripture does not say "and to seeds," meaning many people, but "and to your seed," meaning one person, who is Christ.

Galatians 3:29 If you belong to Christ, then you are Abraham's seed, and heirs according to the promise.

Romans 6:4 We were therefore buried with Him through baptism into death in order that, just as Christ was raised from the dead through the glory of the Father, we too may live a new life.

I Peter 1:3 Praise be to the God and Father of our Lord Jesus Christ! In His great mercy he has given us new birth into a living hope through the resurrection of Jesus Christ from the dead.

We have a different SOURCE!

The Victory

2 Corinthians 5:17 Therefore, if anyone is in Christ, the new creation has come: The old has gone, the new is here.

Colossians 3:3 For you died, and your life is now hidden with Christ in God.

2 Peter 1:3 For His divine power has bestowed upon us all things that [are requisite and suited] to life and godliness.

Galatians 2:20 I have been crucified with Christ and I no longer live, but Christ lives in me. The life I now live in the body, I live by faith in the Son of God, who loved me and gave Himself for me.

Romans 6:6-8 For we know that our old self was crucified with Him so that the body ruled by sin might be done away with, that we should no longer be slaves to sin, because anyone who has died has been set free from sin. Now if we died with Christ, we believe that we will also live with Him.

Power for Victory

ALL THAT HE IS I AM
I Can't but HE CAN!

There is nothing in me for the enemy to condemn!

Colossians 2:9-10 For in Christ all the fullness of the Deity lives in bodily form, and you have been given fullness in Christ,

Colossians 2:13-15 When you were dead in your sins and in the uncircumcision of your flesh, God made you alive with Christ. He forgave us all our sins, having canceled the charge of our legal indebtedness, which stood against us and condemned us; He has taken it away, nailing it to the cross. And having disarmed the powers and authorities, He made a public spectacle of them, triumphing over them by the cross.

Romans 8:1 Therefore, there is now no condemnation for those who are in Christ Jesus,

Look at the next verses together:

Philippians 3:10 I want to know Christ -- yes, to know the power of His resurrection and participation in His sufferings, becoming like him in his death.

Hebrews 2:14 Since the children have flesh and blood, He too shared in their humanity so that by His death He might break the power of him who holds the power of death -- that is, the devil.

Notes:

_____

_____

_____

_____

_____

_____

_____

Power for Victory

THE TRANSFER[1]

FOR HE HAS RESCUED US FROM THE DOMINION OF DARKNESS AND BROUGHT US INTO THE KINGDOM OF THE SON HE LOVES
COLOSSIANS 1:13

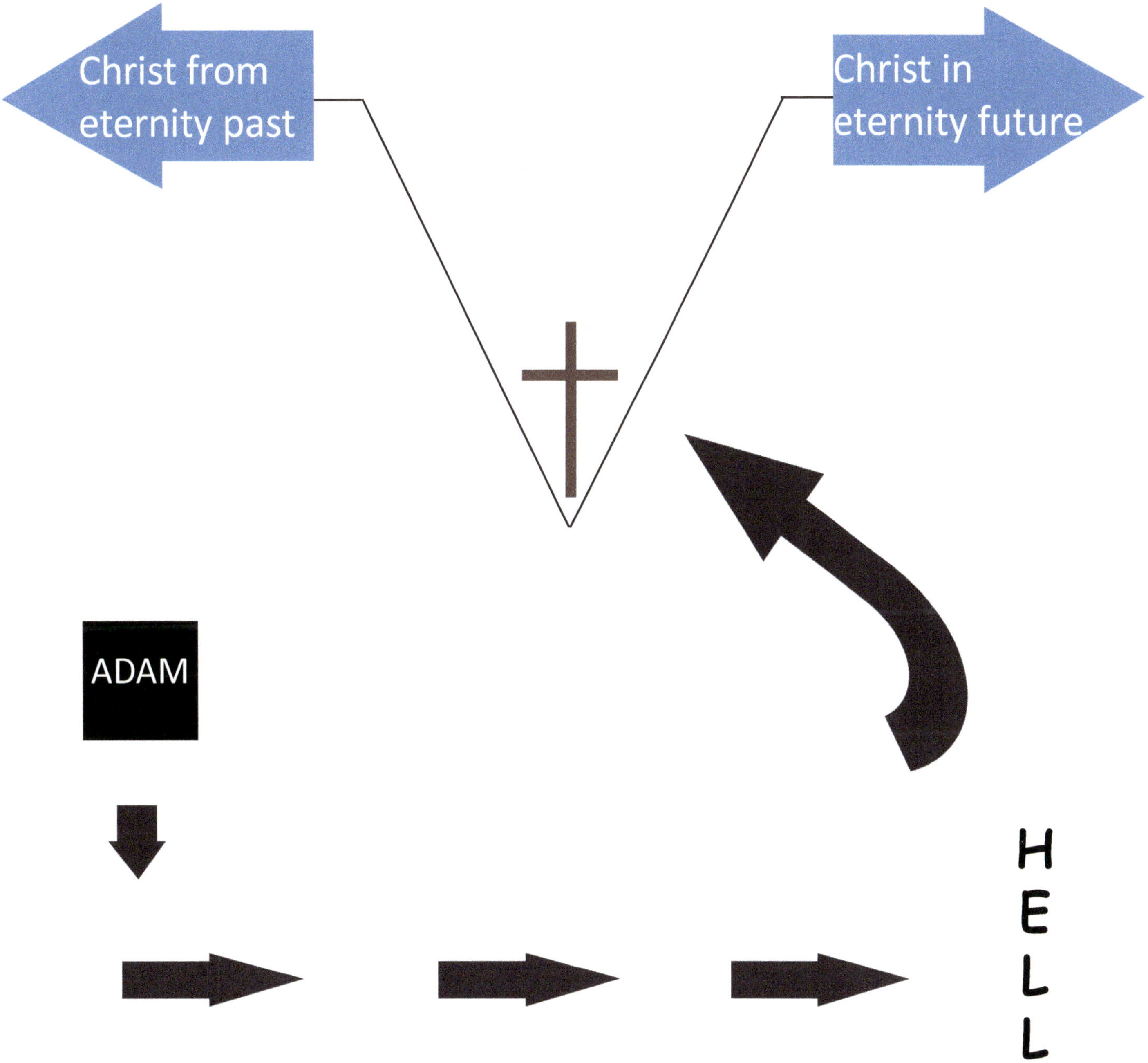

Power for Victory

Responsibilities Regarding the Flesh

What Is the Flesh?

- our false identity
- our ways of relating to God and others pre-salvation
- our ways of coping and protecting ourselves
- ALL THAT I AM APART FROM GOD
- place of strongholds

My Responsibilities

Rid yourselves

Colossians 3:8 But now put away and rid yourselves [completely] of all these things: anger, rage, bad feeling toward others, curses and slander, and foulmouthed abuse and shameful utterances from your lips!

Clothe yourselves

Colossians 3:10 And have clothed yourselves with the new [spiritual self], which is [ever in the process of being] renewed and remolded into [fuller and more perfect knowledge upon] knowledge after the image (the likeness) of Him Who created it.

Colossians 3:12 Clothe yourselves therefore, as God's own chosen ones (His own picked representatives), [who are] purified and holy and well-beloved [by God Himself, by putting on behavior marked by] tenderhearted pity and mercy, kind feeling, a lowly opinion of yourselves, gentle ways, [and] patience [which is tireless and long-suffering, and has the power to endure whatever comes, with good temper].

Consider yourselves

Romans 6:11 Even so consider yourselves also dead to sin and your relation to it broken, but alive to God [living in unbroken fellowship with Him] in Christ Jesus.

Put to death

Romans 8:13 For if you live according to [the dictates of] the flesh, you will surely die. But if through the power of the [Holy] Spirit you are [habitually] putting to death (making extinct, deadening) the [evil] deeds prompted by the body, you shall [really and genuinely] live forever.

Galatians 5:24-25 Those who belong to Christ Jesus have crucified the flesh with its passions and desires. Since we live by the Spirit, let us keep in step with the Spirit.

Colossians 3:5 Put to death, therefore, whatever belongs to your earthly nature: sexual immorality, impurity, lust, evil desires and greed, which is idolatry.

Week Three

Understanding Our Struggle

Open Doors:

Occult, Infirmities, Idolatry, Rebellion, Addictions, Escape, Financial Problems, Mocking, Not Motivated

Week 3: Understanding Our Struggle

Ephesians 6:12
For our struggle is not against flesh and blood, but against the rulers, against the authorities, against the powers of this dark world and against the spiritual forces of evil in the heavenly realms.

The What, the Why and the How
Understanding Spiritual Strongholds

What Is a Stronghold?

What is a stronghold?

Remember it is NOT you!

- Example of Ananias
    - **Acts 5:3** Then Peter said, "Ananias, how is it that Satan has so filled your heart that you have lied to the Holy Spirit and have kept for yourself some of the money you received for the land?
- Splinter
    - **Romans 7:17-18** As it is, it is no longer I myself who do it, but it is sin living in me.

- **Colossians 2:9-10** For in Christ all the fullness of the Deity lives in bodily form, and in Christ you have been brought to fullness.

Why Does Satan Get Entry?

Satan's legal rights - points of entry
- generational curses/bondage
- habitual sin
- unforgiveness
- trauma/traumatic life experiences
- occult

Understanding our Struggle

How Do We Defeat Him?

Colossians 2:23 legalism is of little value in controlling the passions of the flesh.

2 Corinthians 10:4-5 The weapons we fight with are not the weapons of the world. On the contrary, they have divine power to demolish strongholds. We demolish arguments and every pretension that sets itself up against the knowledge of God, and we take captive thought to make it obedient to Christ.

Ephesians 6:10 Be strong in the LORD [be empowered through your union with Him]

2 of our Weapons

Repentance and Forgiveness

- Confess your sins and be cleansed
- Confess to one another and be healed.

I John 1:9 If we confess our sins, He is faithful and just and will forgive us our sins and purify us from all unrighteousness.

James 5:16 Therefore confess your sins to each other and pray for each other so that you may be healed. The prayer of a righteous person is powerful and effective.

James 4:7 Submit yourselves, then, to God. Resist the devil, and he will flee from you.

Sins of the Fathers

The Concept

Exodus 34:6-7 And He passed in front of Moses, proclaiming, "The LORD, the LORD, the compassionate and gracious God, slow to anger, abounding in love and faithfulness, maintaining love to thousands, and forgiving wickedness, rebellion and sin. Yet He does not leave the guilty unpunished; He punishes the children and their children for the sin of the parents to the third and fourth generation.

Iniquity:

A curse:

A blessing:

Understanding our Struggle

Sins of the Fathers
(continued)

Deuteronomy 24:16 Parents are not to be put to death for their children, nor children put to death for their parents; each will die for their own sin.

Exodus 20:4-6 "You shall not make for yourself an image in the form of anything in heaven above or on the earth beneath or in the waters below. You shall not bow down to them or worship them; for I, the LORD your God, am a jealous God, punishing the children for the sin of the parents to the third and fourth generation of those who hate me, but showing love to a thousand generations of those who love me and keep my commandments."

The Solution

Leviticus 26:40-42 "'But if they will confess their sins and the sins of their ancestors-- their unfaithfulness and their hostility toward me, which made me hostile toward them so that I sent them into the land of their enemies--then when their uncircumcised hearts are humbled and they pay for their sin, I will remember my covenant with Jacob and my covenant with Isaac and my covenant with Abraham, and I will remember the land.

Identification Repentance

Daniel 9

Nehemiah 9

Ezra 9

Appropriate the Power of the Cross

Take the cross of Christ and place it between us and past generations

Colossians 2:6 So then, just as you received Christ Jesus as Lord, continue to live your lives in him,

Colossians 2:14 having canceled the charge of our legal indebtedness, which stood against us and condemned us; He has taken it away, nailing it to the cross.

Galatians 3:13 Christ redeemed us from the curse of the law by becoming a curse for us--for it is written, "Cursed is everyone who is hanged on a tree."

Understanding our Struggle

Notes:

Prayer

Prayer for Personal and Generational Sins[2]

1. I confess the sins of my ancestors, my parents and my own sin of _____ including: _____.

2. I specifically confess the following ways/times I have sinned in this area: _____.

3. I choose to repent of this sin. I repent for having received the spirit of _____.

    I ask You to forgive me, Lord, for this sin - for giving it and the resulting curses a place in my life.

4. *I receive your forgiveness. Thank You! On the basis of Your forgiveness I choose to forgive myself for involvement in this sin.

5. I choose to forgive and release those who have hurt me, for the sin, the curses and the consequences in my life. (be specific)

6. I renounce the sin and curses of _____ and I break this power from my life and from the lives of my descendants through the redemptive work of Christ on the cross.

7. I receive God's freedom from this sin and from the resulting curses. I receive _____.

If working with a partner substitute what is below for #4:

*Prayer of ministry partner:
   (Name of person) , God's Word promises "that if we confess our sin, He is faithful and just and will forgive our sins and purify us from all unrighteousness." So I declare to you in Jesus' Name that you are totally forgiven.
   Do you receive God's forgiveness?
   Do you forgive yourself?[3]

Week Four

Repentance/ Forgiveness

"Real" Thoughts on Perfection & Pride

Open Doors:
Performance, Shame, Bound Emotions, Unworthiness, Depression, Emotional Dependency, Failure, Pride, Religion

Week 4: Repentance/Forgiveness

The Role of Repentance

What Is Confession?

Assent, acknowledge, agree fully (with God)

What Is Repentance?

- Think differently, turn around
- It is not remorse

- **2 Corinthians 7:10** Godly sorrow brings repentance that leads to salvation and leaves no regret, but worldly sorrow brings death.
- If we are only reacting to the consequences of our sin we have worldly sorrow
- The more ownership you take, the deeper the freedom gained
- Saying *sorry* isn't enough
- Role of shame

- **1 John 1:10** If we claim we have not sinned, we make Him out to be a liar and His word is not in us.

- Continued sin leads to slavery

- **Romans 6:15-16** What then? Shall we sin because we are not under the law but under grace? By no means! Don't you know that when you offer yourselves to someone as obedient slaves, you are slaves of the one you obey - whether you are slaves to sin, which leads to death, or to obedience, which leads to righteousness?

The Role of Forgiveness

Including the Need, Motive, Demand, Definition, Help, Method, and Follow Through

The Need for Forgiveness

- We are wounded in this life
- Hurting people hurt people

Repentance/Forgiveness

The Need for Forgiveness (cont.)

Jesus Offers an Exchange - wholeness

Isaiah 61:1-3 The Spirit of the Sovereign LORD is on me, because the LORD has anointed me to proclaim good news to the poor. He has sent me to bind up the brokenheared, to proclaim freedom for the captives and release from darkness for the prisoners, to proclaim the year of the LORD's favor and the day of vengeance of our God, to comfort all who mourn, and provide for those who grieve in Zion -- to bestow on them a crown of beauty instead of ashes, the oil of joy instead of mourning, and a garment of praise instead of a spirit of despair.

The Motive for Forgiveness

Jesus died for both the wrongs that we have done and the wrongs done to us.

Isaiah 53:5-6 But He was pierced for our transgressions, He was crushed for our iniquities; the punishment that brought us peace was on Him, and by His wounds we are healed. We all like sheep have gone astray, each of us has turned to our own way; and the LORD has laid on Him the iniquity of us all.

- **Gal 2:21** I do not set aside the grace of God, for if righteousness could be gained through the law, Christ died for nothing!"

- Joseph's Example (Genesis 50:19)

- We forgive for <u>us</u> - we reap what we sow

- Forgiveness <u>unhooks us</u> as we release them, breaking a spiritual tie that enslaves us

God's Demand of Forgiveness

Mark 11:25 And when you stand praying, if you hold anything against anyone, forgive them, so that your Father in heaven may forgive you your sins.

Matthew 18:22 Jesus answered him, I tell you, not up to seven times, but seventy times seven!

Matthew 18:34 And in wrath his master turned him over to the torturers (the jailers), till he should pay all that he owed. So also My heavenly Father will deal with every one of you if you do not freely forgive your brother from your heart his offenses.

Repentance/Forgiveness

The Definition of Forgiveness

- Cancel the debt
- Pardon/forgive without exacting a payment or penalty
- Release/separate yourself from the offender
- Agree to live with the consequences of another person's actions
- Choose not to (want to) hurt those who have hurt you
- Doesn't mean trust
- Is an act of the will not the emotions

The Help for Forgiveness

The Holy Spirit

Romans 8:26 So too the [Holy] Spirit comes to our aid and bears us up in our weakness; for we do not know what prayer to offer nor how to offer it worthily as we ought, but the Spirit Himself goes to meet our supplication and pleads in our behalf with unspeakable yearnings and groanings too deep for utterance... because the Spirit intercedes and pleads [before God] in behalf of the saints according to and in harmony with God's will.

- Understanding the weakness of the person who wounded you
- Understanding that your perception of the event may be clouded by your *filters*
- Understanding your part in the death of Christ and His immense forgiveness
- Know we are fighting against Satan and not the other person, they are the "victims" & tools also

The Method of Forgiveness

- (See the Forgiveness Worksheet included on page 33 in this chapter)
- Ask God to forgive you for your unforgiveness (it is sin)
- Separate the person from the offense
- Give the offense to Jesus to deal with
- Decide to live with the consequences of the other person's sin
- You know you have forgiven when you can say:

    On the day of judgment I will have no accusation against them[4]

- Ask God to bless them
- Release your expectations

Repentance/Forgiveness

The Follow Through of Forgiveness

- Replace ungodly beliefs about yourself/false identity
- Renounce the lie that God is like the person who hurt you
- Develop a heart of compassion - look at the other through the eyes of Jesus
- An offense may be given, but it doesn't have to be <u>received</u>

Notes:

Forgiveness Worksheet

Person	The Offense	How you Felt	What it Cost you

Week 4

Making it Real.

Dealing with Open Doors
Highlight: **Performance, Perfection, Pride**

Real Thoughts on Performance:

- What is the source of Performance?

- What is the role of identity in the midst of Performance?

- What is the role of congruence in the midst of Performance?

- What is the difference between jealousy and envy/covetousness in the midst of Performance?

Real Thoughts on Perfection:

Matthew 5:48 Be perfect, therefore, as your heavenly Father is perfect.

> *Complete (in moral character), of full age,[5] the same inside and out*

- Example of the rich young ruler

- Jesus' Example

Hebrews 2:10 In bringing many sons and daughters to glory, it was fitting that God, for whom and through whom everything exists, should make the pioneer of their salvation perfect through what He suffered.

Hebrews 5:9 and, once made perfect, He became the source of eternal salvation for all who obey him.

Real Thoughts on Pride:

- Self at the center

Week Five

Vows/ Judgments

"Real" Thoughts on Abandonment & Rejection

Open Doors:
Abandonment, Neglect, Orphan Lifestyle, Rejection, Victimization, Anxiety, Death, Identity Issues, Fear

Week 5 — Vows/Judgments

What God Says about Vows and Judgments

Definition of Vow

Vow:

Matthew 5:34 - 37 But I tell you, do not swear an oath at all: either by heaven, for it is God's throne; or by the earth, for it is his footstool; or by Jerusalem, for it is the city of the Great King. And do not swear by your head, for you cannot make even one hair white or black. All you need to say is simply 'Yes' or 'No'; anything beyond this comes from the evil one.

James 5:12 Above all, my brothers and sisters, do not swear--not by heaven or by earth or by anything else. All you need to say is a simple "Yes" or "No." Otherwise you will be condemned.

Definition of Judgment (Judge)

Judge:

What is the cost of our judgment?

A Practical Look

Spiritual Laws/Consequences of Judgments

1) We will be judged

    Matthew 7:1 - 2 "Do not judge, or you too will be judged. For in the same way you judge others, you will be judged, and with the measure you use, it will be measured to you.

2) We will receive that problem again in our lives

    Luke 6:37 - 38 "Do not judge, and you will not be judged. Do not condemn, and you will not be condemned. Forgive, and you will be forgiven. Give, and it will be given to you. A good measure, pressed down, shaken together and running over, will be poured into your lap. For with the measure you use, it will be measured to you."

3) We will begin to be like the person we judge

    Romans 2:1 You, therefore, have no excuse, you who pass judgment on someone else, for at whatever point you judge another, you are condemning yourself, because you who pass judgment do the same things.

Vows/Judgments

Spiritual laws/Consequences of Judgments (cont.)

4) We stand in the place of God

   Romans 14:4 Who are you to judge someone else's servant? To their own master, servants stand or fall. And they will stand, for the Lord is able to make them stand.

5) There is a progression to an orphan heart[6]. Judgment cuts off our inheritance.

   When we judge a parent, we dishonor them, then life will not go well for us in that area.
   Deuteronomy 5:16 "Honor your father and your mother, as the LORD your God has commanded you, so that you may live long and that it may go well with you in the land the LORD your God is giving you.

6) We defile many

   Hebrews 12:15 See to it that no one falls short of the grace of God and that no bitter root grows up to cause trouble and defile many.

7) Our judgments become vows and curses

   James 3:9-10 With the tongue we praise our Lord and Father, and with it we curse human beings, who have been made in God's likeness. Out of the same mouth come praise and cursing. My brothers and sisters, this should not be.

Indicators of Judgments

Statements that may indicate a judgment has been made:

   I would never _____.

   _____ isn't right/is wrong.

   He should, shouldn't...

   That is __(negative assessment)__.

   I can't believe...

   He needs to change (or I will be bothered until he does).

   He/she is/you are so _____.

   You would have thought by now......

Experiences that may indicate judgment is in operation:

   A discerning spirit (a good thing)

   Any areas of discontent

   Any negative similarities of your spouse (or person close to you) to a parent

Vows/Judgments

Indicators of Judgments (cont.)

Experiences that may indicate judgment is in operation (continued):

- Any areas you feel judged
- Any areas you can't get breakthrough or you feel stuck (you keep acting the same way, having the same disappointments, roadblocks, having the same kind of people drive you nuts)
- Any problems that have been duplicated/repeated
- Does a person close to you act contrary to his natural character?

Steps to Freedom

- Ask God to reveal who you judged – it may be yourself
- Ask God if there is any reward you are receiving that keeps you from wanting to repent of the judgment
- Pray through the prayer to break judgments (page 43)
- Renounce each judgmental thought as it comes

Notes:

_____

_____

_____

_____

_____

_____

_____

Prayer

Prayer to Break Judgments

1. I confess my sin and ask You to forgive me, Lord, for judging _____ by thinking/feeling/saying _____.

2. I forgive _____ for any "facts"/offenses which may have precipitated my judgment.

3. I am no longer in agreement with this judgment. I hate it and renounce it. I break and remove the legal rights I gave the enemy to carry out the effects of this judgment.

4. Thank You for the cross and the shed blood of Jesus. I take the cross of Christ and place it between the judgments and _____ and also place it between the judgments and myself.

5. I release the Holy Spirit to meet the need of _____ which is at the core of his/her behavior/attitude. I release healing to him/her.

6. I receive Your healing.

Week 5

Making it Real.

> ## Dealing with Open Doors
> *Highlight:* **Abandonment and Rejection**

Dealing with Abandonment

Psalm 27:10 Though my father and mother forsake me, the LORD will receive me.

Psalm 22:10 From birth I was cast on you; from my mother's womb you have been my God.

> *We need to move from what others have done to what God has done.*

Psalm 62:8 Trust in Him at all times, you people; pour out your hearts to him, for God is our refuge.

Dealing with Rejection

(God's rhema word for me:)

Psalm 71:5-6 For you have been my hope, Sovereign LORD, my confidence since my youth. From birth I have relied on you; you brought me forth from my other's womb. I will ever praise you.

> *We must see the importance of repenting for having RECEIVED a spirit.*

Week Six

Soul Ties

"Real" Thoughts on Anger

Open Doors:
Anger, Bitterness, Deception, Grief, Mental Problems, Trauma, Unbelief, Violence, Control, Sexual Bondage

Week 6 — Soul Ties

What is a Soul Tie?

We Were Created for Godly Unions and Relationships (parent/child; husband/wife)

A Marriage Covenant Is a Healthy Soul Tie

Ephesians 5:31 "For this reason a man will leave his father and mother and be united to his wife, and the two will become one flesh."

An (ungodly) soul tie is an ungodly "knitting together" or covenant with another person. They come from unhealthy (sinful) physical, emotional or spiritual relationships.

Biblical Examples:

David and Jonathan & Ruth and Naomi are examples of Godly soul ties.

I Samuel 18:1-3 After David had finished talking with Saul, Jonathan became one in spirit with David, and he loved him as himself. From that day Saul kept David with him and did not let him return home to his family. And Jonathan made a covenant with David because he loved him as himself.

Ruth 1:14 At this they wept aloud again. Then Orpah kissed her mother-in-law goodbye, but Ruth clung to her.

Soul Tie between Israel and Benjamin

Genesis 44:30-31 "So now, if the boy is not with us when I go back to your servant my father, and if my father, whose life is closely bound up with the boy's life sees that the boy isn't there, he will die."

The Role of Covenant: God Takes Covenants Seriously and Will Not Break Them even if They Were Made with the Enemy

Joshua's covenant with the Gibeonites: Joshua 9:3-27, 2 Samuel 21:1-3

Soul Ties

Ungodly Soul Ties Result from Sinful Sexual Practices and Dysfunctional Relationships

1 Corinthians 6:16 Do you not know that he who unites himself with a prostitute is one with her in body? For it is said, "The two will become one flesh."

Understand the role of the depravity of our day.
See Romans 1.

These ungodly relationships can include relationships with:

- Woman
- Man
- Idol
- Pornographic Image
- Deceased
- Animal
- Spiritual being (incubus and succubus)

Symptoms of ungodly soul ties in relationships:

- Marital difficulties
- Emotional problems (including dominance, passivity, anger/blame, fear)
- Preoccupations
- Relationship Issues

You "marry" the demons of the other person

Steps to Break Soul Ties

- Repent of sexual sins first
- Forgive each person you have been involved with which has resulted in an ungodly soul tie
- Pray the prayer to break soul ties (see next page)
- Be ready to give back any representative gifts you have received
- Set your will to walk in holiness

Prayer

Prayer of Submission and Renouncing Ungodly Soul Ties

I submit myself fully to the authority of the Lord Jesus Christ. I confess and renounce all my ungodly unions and ask You to forgive me for my sins which resulted in ungodly soul ties. Lord, I receive Your forgiveness and I forgive myself. I thank You that I am forgiven and cleansed.

Lord, I sever my ungodly soul ties and union with_____. I forgive him/her. I release myself from him/her and I release him/her from me.
I take back the things I gave (be specific).
I give back the things I took (be specific).
I renounce the covenants/vows which I made.
As I do this, I pray that You would cause him/her to be all that You have intended and that I would also be all that You intended for me.

I renounce every soul tie and break every authority I've given to the demonic to operate because of this relationship. I bind all powers of darkness that came through this ungodly soul tie (you may be specific here) and I command you to go where Jesus sends you.

I place the blood of Jesus between myself each person I've named.
I renounce and cancel the assignments of all evil spirits sent to maintain these ungodly unions and soul ties.

Lord, please cleanse my mind and emotions from all ungodly unions. Fill these areas with Your presence and Holy Spirit. Thank You for restoring me to wholeness.

Soul Ties

Notes:

Week 6

Making it Real.

Dealing with Open Doors
Highlight: **Anger**

1. The Role of Goals

2. The Role of Interpretation (lies)

3. The Anger Ladder

1. Seeking resolution
2. Pleasant behavior
3. Focusing anger on source only
4. Holding to the primary complaint
5. Thinking logically and constructively
6. Unpleasant and loud behavior
7. Cursing
8. Displacing anger to sources other than the original
9. Expressing unrelated complaints
10. Throwing objects
11. Destroying property
12. Verbal abuse
13. Emotionally destructive behavior
14. Physical abuse
15. Passive-aggressive behavior

The Anger Ladder is taken from *How to Really Love your Teenager* by Ross Campbell, MD[7]

Week Seven

Renewing the Mind

"Real" Thoughts on Rebellion

Activation:
Renewing the Mind

Week 7: Renewing the Mind

Changing Our Belief System is Necessary for Victory

Ungodly Beliefs Are:
- beliefs
- attitudes
- understandings
- expectations

*about ourselves, others or God

* that are not in agreement with God (His nature/character or His Word)

The Process of Renewing Your Mind

2 Corinthians 10:5 We demolish arguments and every pretension that sets itself up against the knowledge of God, and we take captive every thought to make it obedient to Christ.

Romans 12:2 Do not conform to the pattern of this world, but be transformed by the renewing of your mind. Then you will be able to test and approve what God's will is -- His good, pleasing and perfect will.

> **We discover our ungodly beliefs by our reactions/ behaviors/feelings, not by what we say we think.**

The Role of Interpretation

The lies we believe:[8]

The spirit of 'wrong focus'[9]

The problem of ingratitude

To renew the mind, understand the difference between:
- Fact and Truth[10]
- Circumstances and Reality

The concept of waiting

Renewing the Mind

The Belief-Expectation Cycle[11]

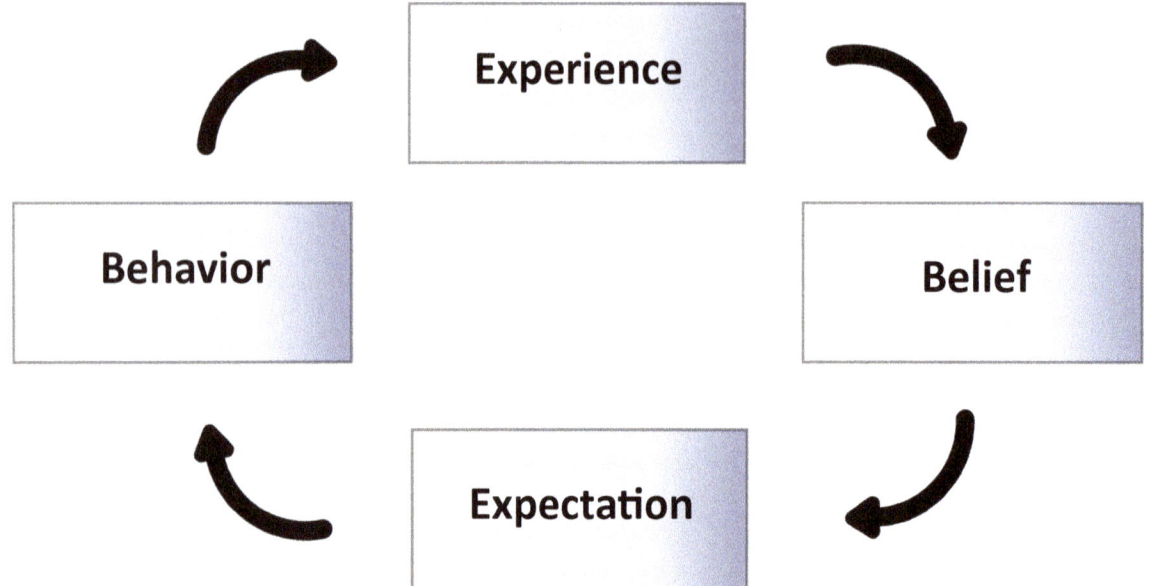

Belief System (by Anonymous)[12]

If you accept a belief,
You reap a thought.

If you sow a Thought,
You reap an attitude.

If you sow an attitude,
You reap an action.

If you sow an action,
You reap a habit.

If you sow a habit,
You reap a character.

If you sow a character,
You reap a destiny.

*Concepts of The Belief-Expectation Cycle are taken from RTF

Renewing the Mind

Notes:

Prayer

Prayer for Ungodly Beliefs [13]

1. I confess my sin and my ancestor's sin (if appropriate) of believing the lie that_____ _____.

2. I forgive those who modeled this, who provoked me to believe this, or who were responsible for circumstances that led me to form this ungodly belief. I specifically forgive _____ for _____ that made me feel_____ and cost me _____.

3. I ask You to forgive me Lord, for receiving this ungodly belief, for living my life based on it and for all the ways I have judged others because of it. I receive Your forgiveness.

4. Because You have forgiven me, Lord, I will forgive myself for believing this lie.

5. I renounce this ungodly belief and break my agreement with it.

STOP to formulate the Godly belief.

6. I choose to accept, believe and receive the Godly belief that _____.

Godly beliefs should be brief, stick to the primary issue, use positive language and not be so 'spiritual' that they will stay in the person's head and not heart. They should be relevant and believable.

Renewing the Mind

THE FOLLOWING UNGODLY BELIEFS ARE TAKEN DIRECTLY FROM RESTORING THE FOUNDATIONS[14]

UNGODLY BELIEFS ABOUT MYSELF:
Read the following statements, and check (✓) the ones that you relate to or agree with.
Please make adjustments or alterations to any of the words to help make the belief fit you.

Theme: Rejection, Not Belonging

____1. I don't belong. I will always be on the outside (left out).
____2. My feelings don't count. No one cares what I feel.
____3. No one will love me or care about me just for myself.
____4. I will always be lonely. The special man (woman) in my life will not be there for me.
____5. _____

Theme: Unworthiness, Guilt, Shame

____1. I am not worthy to receive anything from God.
____2. I am the problem. When something is wrong, it is my fault.
____3. I am a bad person. If you knew the real me, you would reject me.
____4. I must wear a mask so that people won't find out how horrible I am and reject me.
____5. I have messed up so badly that I have missed God's best for me.
____6. _____

Theme: Doing to Achieve Self-Worth, Value, Recognition

____1. I will never get credit for what I do.
____2. My value is in what I do. I am valuable because I do good to others.
____3. Even when I do/give my best, it is not good enough. I can never meet the standard.
____4. God doesn't care if I have a 'secret life', as long as I appear to be good.
____5. _____

Theme: Control (to avoid hurt)

____1. I have to plan every day of my life. I have to continually plan/strategize. I can't relax.
____2. The perfect life is one in which no conflict is allowed and so there is peace.
____3. I will isolate myself so that I won't be vulnerable to hurt, rejection, etc., any more.
____4. I will choose to be passive in order to avoid conflict that would risk others' disapproval.
____5. _____

Theme: Physical

____1. I am unattractive. God shortchanged me.
____2. I am doomed to have certain physical disabilities. They are just part of what I have inherited.
____3. It is impossible to lose weight (or gain weight). I am just stuck.
____4. _____

Theme: Personality Traits

____1. I will always be _____ (angry, shy, jealous, insecure, fearful, etc.)
____2. I will never be _____ (likable, lovable, happy, safe, content, etc.)
____3. _____

Renewing the Mind

Theme: Identity

____1. I should have been a boy ____ girl ____. Then my parents would have valued/loved me more.
____2. Men ____ Women ____ have it better.
____3. I am not complete as a man ___ woman ____.
____4. I will never be known or appreciated for my real self.
____5. I will never really change and be as God wants me to be.
____6. _____

Theme: Miscellaneous

____1. I have wasted a lot of time and energy, some of my best years.
____2. Turmoil is normal for me.
____3. I will always have financial problems.
____4. I just don't have the (time, energy, resources, _____) to fully follow God.
____5. _____

Theme: Sonship

____1. No one will ever love me enough to take care of me.
____2. Other people don't meet my standards so I must do it myself.
____3. It's not safe to submit myself to someone else.
____4. The best way to survive is to (___avoid, ___overpower) other people.
____5. I'm a victim of my circumstances and there is no hope of change.
____6. I'm all alone.
____7. I will always need to be strong in order to protect and defend myself.
____8. Something is wrong with me.
____9. The significant people in my life are not there for me and will not be there when I need them.
____10. I will never be a priority with those in authority over me.
____11. _____

UNGODLY BELIEFS ABOUT OTHERS:

Theme: Safety/Protection

____1. I must be very guarded about what I say, since anything I say may be used against me.
____2. I have to guard and hide my emotions and feelings.
____3. I cannot give anyone the satisfaction of knowing that they have wounded or hurt me. I will not be vulnerable, humiliated, or shamed.
____4. _____

Theme: Retaliation

____1. The correct way to respond if someone offends me is to punish them by withdrawing and/or cutting them off.
____2. I will make sure that _____ hurts as much as I hurt!
____3. _____

Renewing the Mind

Theme: Victim

___ 1. Authority figures will humiliate me and violate me.
___ 2. I will always be used and abused by other people.
___ 3. My value is based totally on others' judgment/perception about me..
___ 4. I am completely under their authority. I have no will or choice of my own.
___ 5. I will not be known, understood, loved or appreciated for who I am by those close to me.
___ 6. _____

Theme: Hopelessness/Helplessness

___ 1. I am out there all alone. If I get into trouble or need help, there is no one to rescue me.
___ 2. I have made such a mess of my life there is no use going on.
___ 3. _____

Theme: Defective in Relationships

___ 1. I will never be able to fully give or receive love. I don't know what it is.
___ 2. If I let anyone get close to me, I may get my heart broken again. I can't let myself risk it.
___ 3. If I fail to please you, I won't receive your pleasure and acceptance of me.
___ 4. I must strive (perfectionism) to do whatever is necessary to try to please you.
___ 5. _____

Theme: God

___ 1. God loves other people more than He loves me.
___ 2. God only values me for what I do. My life is just a means to an end.
___ 3. No matter how much I try, I'll never be able to do enough nor do it well enough to please God.
___ 4. God is judging me when I relax. I have to stay busy about His work or He will abandon me.
___ 5. God has let me down before. He may do it again. I can't trust Him or feel secure with Him.
___ 6. _____

Other ungodly beliefs I relate to or agree with:

_____

_____

_____

_____

Week 7

Making it Real.

Dealing with Open Doors
Highlight: **Rebellion**

Look for the root and not at just the behavior. Then determine what the "other side" is.

Behavior	Root Cause	"Other Side"
Anger		
Rebellion		
Control		
Addictions		
Victim		

Dealing with Rebellion

1 Samuel 15:23 But when you ask, you must believe and not doubt, because the one who doubts is like a wave of the sea, blown and tossed by the wind.

1 Peter 2:13-15 Submit yourselves for the Lord's sake to every human authority: whether to the emperor, as the supreme authority, or to governors, who are sent by him to punish those who do wrong and to commend those who do right. For it is God's will that by doing good you should silence the ignorant talk of foolish people.

Matthew 5:41 If anyone forces you to go one mile, go with them two miles.

The attitude you have toward authorities is the attitude you have toward God.

Philippians 2:6 Who, although being essentially one with God and in the form of God [*possessing the fullness of the attributes which make God God*], did not think this equality with God was a thing to be eagerly grasped or retained.

Ephesians 5:21 Submit to one another out of reverence for Christ.

Week Eight

The Shame, Fear, Control Connection

"Real" Thoughts on Fear and Unbelief

Activation:
Renewing the Mind

Week 8: The Shame, Fear, Control Connection

> A 3-CD set for further teaching and practical exercise is available for purchase from www.rtfi.org.

Two problems unique to the Shame stronghold:
- *It is the nature of shame to hide*
- *The shaming event is usually not my fault*

A Look at Shame

What is shame?

    Chester & Betsy Kylstra state shame says:
        "*I am uniquely and hopelessly flawed.*"[15]

Where does shame come from?

How does shame manifest?

    Our shame preprograms us in how to interpret/respond to our circumstances.

A Testimony of Progressive Healing

A Testimony:

    Being healed from shame was a progression.
    It is important to find God's presence in the trauma.

    Psalm 27:10 Although my father and mother forsake me the Lord will take me up.

    Psalm 22:10 I was cast upon You from my birth, from my mother's womb You have been my God.

The Shame, Fear, Control Connection

Fear and Control as a Results of Shame

What happens when we react from a core of shame:

1. We walk in FEAR

    How does this manifest?

> **CONFESSING MY SIN DOES NOT DESTROY MY IDENTITY**

2. We walk in CONTROL

    All control is to protect

    How does this manifest?

What happens when one has dealt with shame but not recognized fear?

We Must Deal with These Strongholds Together

Dealing with the Super Stronghold

Separate the strongholds from each other and deal with them one by one, beginning with shame.[16]

Exchange your false identity for a true one.

The Shame, Fear, Control Connection

Basic Lies that Enable the SFC Stronghold[17]

Copyright 1994 Restoring the Foundations Publishing, used by permission

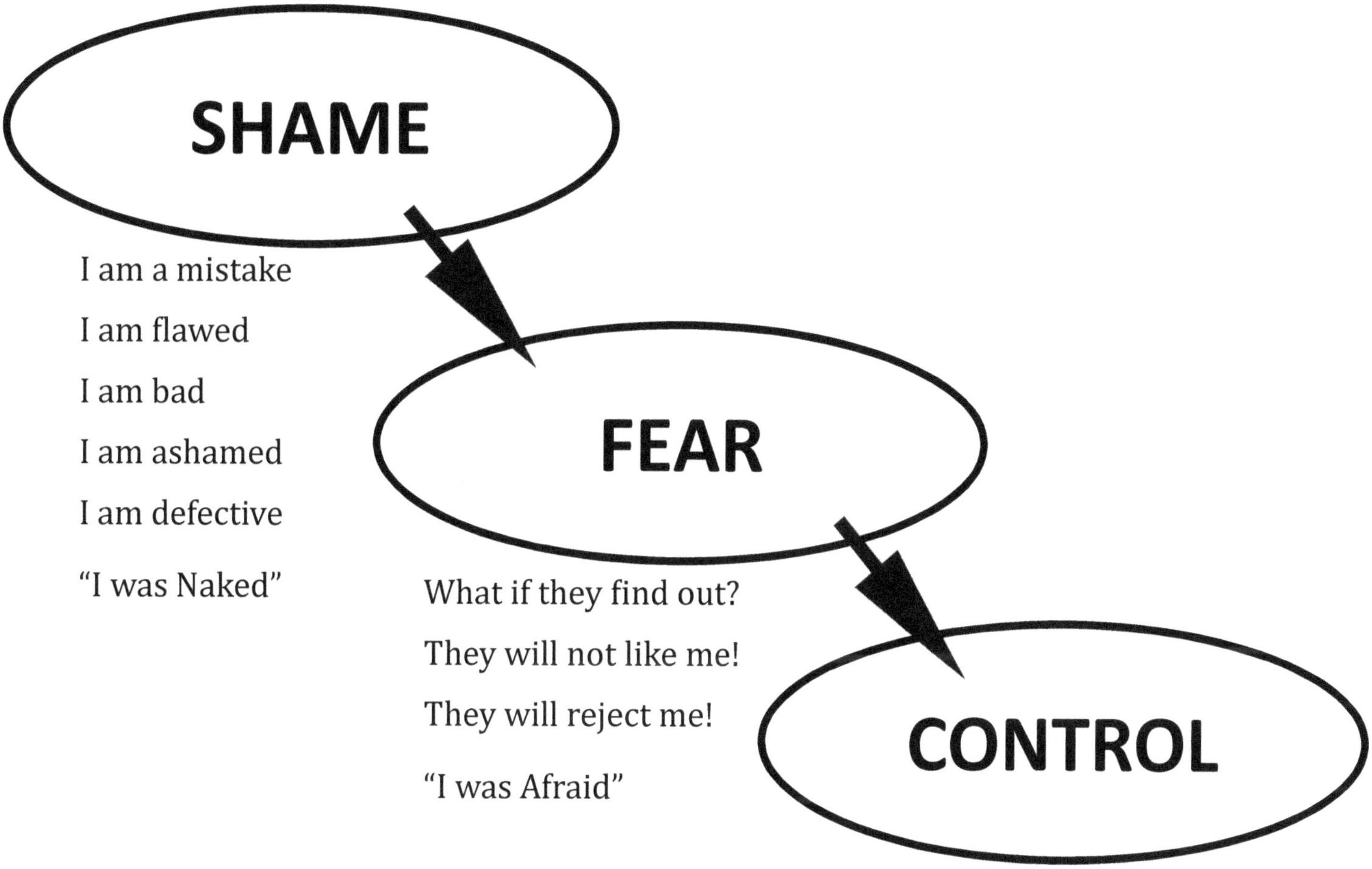

SHAME

I am a mistake
I am flawed
I am bad
I am ashamed
I am defective

"I was Naked"

FEAR

What if they find out?
They will not like me!
They will reject me!

"I was Afraid"

CONTROL

I'll control everything so that they won't find out what I am really like and so I will not get hurt nor suffer pain.

"I hid Myself"

Genesis 3:10

The Shame, Fear, Control Connection

Notes:

Week 8

Making it Real.

> ## Dealing with Open Doors
> *Highlight:* **Fear and Unbelief**

Real Thoughts on Fear

I John 4:18 There is no fear in love. But perfect love drives out fear, because fear has to do with punishment. The one who fears is not made perfect in love.

2 Sources/Motivating Factors: Fear or Love

The cross is proof enough of God's goodness.

What do we do with the emotions of fear?

Real Thoughts on Unbelief

- *Head Knowledge Vs. Faith*
    Unbelief is: Faithless, Unfaithful ?

- *Look at what is listed under unbelief in the open door list*

- *I must release God to be bigger than me*

- *The problem of double-mindedness in unbelief:*

James 1:6 - 8 But when you ask, you must believe and not doubt, because the one who doubts is like a wave of the sea, blown and tossed by the wind. That person should not expect to receive anything from the Lord. Such a person is double-minded and unstable in all they do.

- *Faith is jumping without knowing where we will land*

- *When we begin to reason instead of obeying we are operating out of faithlessness*

Week Nine

Healing Wounds/ Memories of the Past

Activation:

Wounds of the Past

Week 9 Healing Wounds/Memories of the Past

It's Possible to Be Healed!

Psalm 34:18 The LORD is close to the brokenhearted and saves those who are crushed in spirit.
Psalm 147:3 He heals the brokenhearted and binds up their wounds.

Isaiah 61:1 The Spirit of the Sovereign LORD is on me, because the LORD has anointed me to proclaim good news to the poor. He has sent me to bind up the brokenhearted, to proclaim freedom for the captives and release from darkness for the prisoners.

Psalm 23:3 He refreshes and restores my soul.

> **Memories that haven't been healed still hold pain (whether we feel it or not).**

God often heals both specific memories as well as representative ones.

An unhealed memory often has an attachment to an ungodly belief or unforgiveness, judgment, etc.

The facts don't change - but our peace, our understanding, our responses, etc., do change.

God is Eternal, and Outside of Time. He is Ever-present.

Hebrews 13:8 Jesus Christ is the same yesterday and today and forever.
Psalm 139:7-10 Where can I go from Your Spirit? Where can I flee from Your Presence? If I go up to the heaven, You are there; if I make my bed in the depths, You are there. Even there Your hand will guide me, Your right hand will hold me fast.

Healing Wounds/Memories of the Past

> **We are told we can pour out our hearts to God. Holding on to negative emotions will block healing. Don't let shame, fear or control keep you from getting real.**

Psalm 62:8 Trust in Him at all times, you people; pour out your hears to Him, for our God is our refuge.

There is an ungodly belief that Christians shouldn't express negative emotions - and with that ungodly belief is the fear of reprisal in expressing them.

Notes:

_____
_____
_____
_____
_____
_____
_____
_____
_____
_____

Healing Wounds/Memories of the Past

I Told God I was Angry [18]

by Jessica Shaver

I told God I was angry; I thought He'd be surprised
I thought I'd keep hostility quite cleverly disguised.

I told the Lord I hate Him; I told Him that I hurt.
I told Him that He isn't fair, He's treated me like dirt.

I told God I was angry, But I'm the one surprised;
"What I've known all along," He said, "You've finally realized.

"At last you have admitted what's really in your heart:
Dishonesty, not anger, was keeping us apart

Even when you hate Me, I don't stop loving you.
Before you can receive that love, you must confess what's true.

"In telling me the anger you genuinely feel,
It lost its power over you permitting you to heal"

I told God I was sorry, and He's forgiven me.
The truth that I was angry - Had finally set me free.

Prayer

Wounds of the Past Ministry Process

- Submission prayer
- Ask the Holy Spirit to reveal the memory He wants to heal
    - The first memory of the hurt You want to heal or
        - The first memory that contains the root or starting point of _____
    - Clarify the memory by asking questions
    - Encourage ministry receiver to share what he hears/sees/feels. Encourage him to "stay in the memory"
    - Stick with one memory
    - You may need to bind specific spirits: e.g. mind-blocking, confusion, control, etc.
- Express your emotions- - pour out your heart to God
    - You may need to forgive and/or ask for forgiveness
    - Be alert to issues (e.g. ungodly beliefs, vows or judgments) that should be dealt with then or later
- Invite Jesus into the picture. Ask Him how He wants to heal the hurt
    - Give Him plenty of time to bring healing
    - Never tell Jesus or ministry receiver what to do
    - Don't be <u>thinking</u> through the healing, listen for the Holy Spirit and receive. Be watchful for control
    - If "Jesus" does not seem to agree with the character of God or feels wrong in your spirit, have the ministry receiver ask Jesus to bow the knee to the Name of Jesus and declare that Jesus is Lord
- Ask Jesus is there is anything else He wants to say/do
- Return to the memory to see if the pain is gone

Week Ten

Defeating Our Enemy

Activation:

Cast Out

All Open Doors

Week 10 — Defeating Our Enemy

How to Deal with Demons

Foundational Thoughts for Dealing with Demons

1. Position
Ephesians 2:6 And God raised us up with Christ and seated us with Him in the heavenly realms in Christ Jesus,

Ephesians 1:20 - 22 He raised Christ from the dead and seated Him at His right hand in the heavenly realms, far above all rule and authority, power and dominion, and every name that is invoked, not only in the present age but also in the one to come. And God placed all things under His feet and appointed Him to be head over everything for the church.

2. Victory
1 Corinthians 15:57-58 But thanks be to God! He gives us the victory through our Lord Jesus Christ. Therefore, my dear brothers and sisters, stand firm. Let nothing move you.

I John 5:4 for everyone born of God overcomes the world. This is the victory that has overcome the world, even our faith.

Revelation 12:11 They triumphed over him by the blood of the Lamb and by the word of their testimony; they did not love their lives so much as to shrink from death.

Philippians 1:28 without being frightened in any way by those who oppose you. This is a (clear) sign to them that they will be destroyed, but that you will be saved--and that by God.

Romans 16:20 The God of peace will soon crush Satan under your feet.

3. Authority
Matthew 10:1 Jesus called His twelve disciples to Him and gave them authority to drive out impure spirits and to heal every disease and sickness.

Matthew 28:18-19 Then Jesus came to them and said, "All authority in heaven and earth has been given to me. Therefore..."

Mark 3:15 and to have authority to drive out demons.

4. Power (not strength)
I John 4:4 You, dear children, are from God and have overcome them, because the one who is in you is greater than the one who is in the world.

Romans 1:16 For I am not ashamed of the gospel, because it is the power of God that brings salvation to everyone who believes.

5. Sonship
Isaiah 54:17 "no weapon formed against you will prevail, and you will refute every tongue that accuses you. This is the heritage of the servants of the LORD, and this is their vindication from me, "declares the LORD.

Defeating Our Enemy

Foundational Thoughts for Dealing with Demons (cont.)

5. Sonship (continued)

Proverbs 26:2 Like a fluttering sparrow or a darting swallow, an undeserved curse does not come to rest.

1Peter 3:9 Do not repay evil with evil or insult with insult. On the contrary, repay evil with blessing, because to this you were called so that you may inherit a blessing.

2Chronicles 20:21-22 After consulting the people, Jehoshaphat appointed men to sing to the LORD and to praise him for the splendor of his holiness as they went out at the head of the army, saying: "Give thanks to the LORD, for his love endures forever." As they began to sing and praise, the LORD set ambushes against the men of Ammon and Moab and Mount Seir who were invading Judah, and they were defeated.

The Key of My House [19]

Matthew 12:44-45 Then it says, I will go back to my house from which I came out. And when it arrives, it finds the place unoccupied, swept, put in order, and decorated. Then it goes and brings with it seven other spirits more wicked than itself, and they go in and make their home there. And the last condition of that man becomes worse than the first. So also shall it be with this wicked generation.

Our Task

Jesus came to bring life and destroy the works of the devil and we have the commission to cast out devils.

John 10:10 The thief comes only to steal and kill and destroy; I have come that they may have life, and have it to the full.

I John 3:8 The reason the Son of God appeared was to destroy the devil's work.

Mark 16:17 And these signs will accompany those who believe: In my name they will drive out demons.

Important Points

1. The person must be a Christian.
2. If a spirit manifests we can tell it to be quiet and forbid any excessive manifestations, telling the person to take control of his body.
3. It is imperative to have the cooperation of the person - he must want to be free.
4. We can bind a spirit, but should not cast it out if the legal rights have not been dealt with.
5. Should command all demons/spirits to separate from each other.
6. MAKE SURE OPEN DOORS HAVE BEEN DEALT WITH - especially unforgiveness, curses, vows, personal and generational sin.

Prayer

Prayer of Authority over Demons

In the Name of Jesus, I <u>renounce</u> the spirit of _____, including all associated demons of _____. I <u>break the power</u>/bondage of this spirit in my life. I take authority over and <u>cast out</u> the spirit of _____ and I command you to leave me now - in the Name of Jesus and based on His shed blood.

I command all the demons to go to where Jesus sends you and not to return.

Thank you Jesus.

I pray for an infilling of the Holy Spirit.

Defeating Our Enemy

Notes:

Week Eleven

Week of Modeling

Activation:

Wounds of the Past

Week 11 — Week of Modeling

Understanding the Complete Model

Teaching Time Replaced by Observation

Week of Modeling

Notes:

Week Twelve

Keys to Walking in Victory

Keys to Walking in Victory

Week 12

How to Walk It Out

Not Expecting Perfection

1 John 3:2 Dear friends, now we are children of God, and what we will be has not yet been made known. But we know that when Christ appears, we shall be like him, for we shall see him as he is.

*Remember to walk in grace

*Walk in hope and expectation

> We will not take the land in a single day.
> PROCLAIM IT UNTIL YOU SEE IT

We Are Not Promised That Things Will Be Easy

1 Peter 1:7 These things have come so that the proven genuineness of your faith - of greater worth than gold, which perishes even though refined by fire - may result in praise, glory and honor when Jesus Christ is revealed.

John 16:33 "I have told you these things, so that in me you may have peace. In this world you will have trouble. But take heart! I have overcome the world."

James 1:2 Consider it pure joy, my brothers and sisters, whenever you face trials of many kinds; look at trials as an opportunity, with expectation.

Romans 8:1 Therefore, there is now no condemnation for those who are in Christ Jesus.

Romans 8:18 I consider that our present sufferings are not worth comparing with the glory that will be revealed in us.

Romans 8:28 And we know that in all things God works for the good of those who love him, who have been called according to His purpose.

Remember Where the Battle Is - Remember Your Source

ALL THAT HE IS I AM

Galatians 5:16 So I say, walk by the Spirit, and you will not gratify the desires of the flesh.

Ephesians 6:13 Therefore put on the full armor of God, so that when the day of evil comes, you may be able to stand your ground, and <u>after you have done everything, to stand</u>.

Keys to Walking in Victory

Be Assured of Victory

Remember from where you are living

1 Peter 5:7-9 Casting the whole of your care [*all your anxieties, all your worries, all your concerns, once and for all*] on Him for He cares for you affectionately and cares about you watchfully. [Psalm 55:22] Be well balanced (temperate, sober of mind), be vigilant and cautious at all times; for that enemy of yours, the devil, roams around like a lion roaring [*in fierce hunger*], seeking some one to seize upon and devour. Withstand him; be firm in faith against his onset--rooted, established, strong, immovable, and determined],

God is able

Jude 1:24 To Him who is able to keep you from stumbling and to present you before His glorious presence without fault and with great joy.

Philippians 1:6 And I am convinced and sure of this very thing, that He Who began a good work in you will continue until the day of Jesus Christ [*right up to the time of His return*], developing [*that good work*] and perfecting and bringing it to full completion in you.

> **Remember, you can't, but He can**
> **He IS coming for a SPOTLESS bride**

Walk in Gratitude

1 Thessalonians 5:18 Give thanks in all circumstances; for this is God's will for you in Christ Jesus.

Ecclesiastes 3:11 He has made everything beautiful in its time.

Romans 5:10 For if, while we were God's enemies, we were reconciled to Him through the death of His Son, **how much more**, having been reconciled, shall we be saved through His life!

Prayers

Prayer for Personal and Generational Sins[2]

1. I confess the sins of my ancestors, my parents and my own sin of _____,
   including: _____.

2. I specifically confess the following ways/times I have sinned in this area: _____.
   Be specific as you confess: can you remember the first time you sinned in this way? If this is a stronghold in your life ask the Hoy Spirit to help you remember the different events, the people affected and the consequences of your sin.

3. I choose to repent of this sin. I repent for having received the spirit of _____. I ask You to forgive me, Lord, for this sin - for giving it and the resulting curses a place in my life.

4. *I receive your forgiveness. Thank You! On the basis of Your forgiveness I choose to forgive myself for involvement in this sin.

5. I choose to forgive and release those who have hurt me, for the sin, the curses and the consequences in my life. (be specific)
   I forgive ___(name)___ , for ___(the offense)___ , which made me feel _____, and cost me _____.
   I give this person and his sins to God and from now on I will not have any accusation against him.
   Ask the Holy Spirit to reveal who you need to forgive. Who modeled this sin/behavior and /or who brought it into your life? Can you give the pain to Jesus?
   Remember the role of judgment which holds unforgiveness in place. Renounce specific judgments against those you are forgiving.)

6. I renounce the sin and curses of _____ and I break this power from my life and from the lives of my descendants in the Name of Jesus. (through the redemptive work of Christ on the cross.)

7. I receive God's freedom from this sin and from the resulting curses. I receive _____.

If working with a partner substitute what is below for #4:

*Prayer of ministry partner:
   (Name of person), God's Word promises "that if we confess our sin, He is faithful and just and will forgive our sins and purify us from all unrighteousness." So I declare to you in Jesus' Name that you are totally forgiven.
   Do you receive God's forgiveness?
   Do you forgive yourself?[3]

Prayer from Week 3 - Understanding our Struggle - pg. 25

Prayer to Break Judgments

1. I confess my sin and ask You to forgive me, Lord, for judging _____ by thinking/feeling/saying _____.

2. I forgive _____ for any "facts"/offenses which may have precipitated my judgment.

3. I am no longer in agreement with this judgment. I hate it and renounce it. I break and remove the legal rights I gave the enemy to carry out the effects of this judgment.

4. Thank You for the cross and the shed blood of Jesus. I take the cross of Christ and place it between the judgments and _____ and also place it between the judgments and myself.

5. I release the Holy Spirit to meet the need of _____ which is at the core of his/her behavior/attitude. I release healing to him/her.

6. I receive Your healing.

Prayer from Week 5 - Vows/Judgments - pg. 43

Prayer of Submission and Renouncing Ungodly Soul Ties

I submit myself fully to the authority of the Lord Jesus Christ. I confess and renounce all my ungodly unions and ask You to forgive me for my sins which resulted in ungodly soul ties. Lord, I receive Your forgiveness and I forgive myself. I thank You that I am forgiven and cleansed.

Lord, I sever my ungodly soul ties and union with_____. I forgive him/her.
I release myself from him/her and I release him/her from me.
I take back the things I gave (be specific).
I give back the things I took (be specific).
I renounce the covenants/vows which I made.
As I do this, I pray that You would cause him/her to be all that You have intended and that I would also be all that You intended for me.

I renounce every soul tie and break every authority I've given to the demonic to operate because of this relationship. I bind all powers of darkness that came through this ungodly soul tie (you may be specific here) and I command you to go where Jesus sends you.

I place the blood of Jesus between myself each person I've named.
I renounce and cancel the assignments of all evil spirits sent to maintain these ungodly unions and soul ties.

Lord, please cleanse my mind and emotions from all ungodly unions. Fill these areas with Your presence and Holy Spirit. Thank You for restoring me to wholeness.

Prayer from Week 6 - Soul Ties - pg. 51

Prayer for Ungodly Beliefs[13]

1. I confess my sin and my ancestor's sin (if appropriate) of believing the lie that _____.

2. I forgive those who modeled this, who provoked me to believe this, or who were responsible for circumstances that led me to form this ungodly belief. I specifically forgive _____ for _____ that made me feel _____ and cost me _____.

3. I ask You to forgive me Lord, for receiving this ungodly belief, for living my life based on it and for all the ways I have judged others because of it. I receive Your forgiveness.

4. Because You have forgiven me, Lord, I will forgive myself for believing this lie.

5. I renounce this ungodly belief and break my agreement with it.

STOP to formulate the Godly belief.

6. I choose to accept, believe and receive the Godly belief that _____ _____.

Godly beliefs should be brief, stick to the primary issue, use positive language and not be so 'spiritual' that they will stay in the person's head and not heart. They should be relevant and believable.

Prayer from Week 7 - Renewing the Mind - pg. 61

Wounds of the Past Ministry Process

- Submission prayer
- Ask the Holy Spirit to reveal the memory He wants to heal
    The first memory of the hurt You want to heal or
        The first memory that contains the root or starting point of _____
    Clarify the memory by asking questions
    Encourage ministry receiver to share what he hears/sees/feels. Encourage him to "stay in the memory"
    Stick with one memory
    You may need to bind specific spirits: ie, mind-blocking, confusions, control, etc.
- Express your emotions- - pour out your heart to God
    You may need to forgive and/or ask for forgiveness
    Be alert to issues (ie. ungodly beliefs, vows or judgments) that should be dealt with then or later
- Invite Jesus into the picture. Ask Him how He wants to heal the hurt
    Give Him plenty of time to bring healing
    Never tell Jesus or ministry receiver what to do
    Don't be <u>thinking</u> through the healing, listen for the Holy Spirit and receive. Be watchful for control
    If "Jesus" does not seem to agree with the character of God or feels wrong in your spirit, have the ministry receiver ask Jesus to bow the knee to the Name of Jesus and declare that Jesus is Lord
- Ask Jesus is there is anything else He wants to say/do
- Return to the memory to see if the pain is gone

Prayer from Week 9 - Healing the Wounds/Memories of the Past - pg. 83

Prayer of Authority over Demons

In the Name of Jesus, I <u>renounce</u> the spirit of _____, including all associated demons of _____. I <u>break the power</u>/bondage of this spirit in my life. I take authority over and <u>cast out</u> the spirit of _____ and I command you to leave me now - in the Name of Jesus and based on His shed blood.

I command all the demons to go to where Jesus sends you and not to return.

Thank you Jesus.

I pray for an infilling of the Holy Spirit.

Prayer from Week 10 - Defeating our Enemy - pg. 89

Open Doors

THE FOLLOWING PAGES OF OPEN DOORS ARE TAKEN DIRECTLY FROM RESTORING THE FOUNDATIONS [20]

OPEN DOORS

Please put a check mark (√) **only** under the A (Ancestors) column if you know about, or have observed any of these characteristics, events or involvement in your immediate, extended, and/or **ancestral** family line.

However, if any of these apply to you personally, in the S (Self) column put **only** 'C' for current or 'P' for past.

SONSHIP INDICATORS

A S

ABANDONMENT
- Abdication
- Blocked Intimacy
- Desertion
- Divorce
- Emotional Abandonment
- Isolation
- Loneliness
- Neglect
- Not Wanted
- Rejection
- Self-Pity
- Separation
- Unprotected
- _____

ANGER
- Abandonment
- Disappointment
- Intolerance
- Irritability
- Feuding
- Frustration
- Hatred
- Hostility
- Murder
- Punishment
- Rage
- Resentment
- Retaliation
- Revenge
- Spoiled Little Boy/Girl
- Temper Tantrums
- Violence
- _____

BOUND EMOTIONS
- Blocked Emotions
- Hindered Emotions
- Numbness
- Suppressed Emotions
- _____

NEGLECT
- Conditional Love
- Lack of Affirmation
- Lack of Communication
- Lack of Encouragement
- Lack of Guidance
- Lack of Intimacy
- Lack of Love
- Lack of Nurture
- Lack of Protection
- Lack of Security
- _____

A S

ORPHAN LIFESTYLE
- Disconnected
- Discontent
- Dissatisfaction
- Fatherlessness
- Homelessness
- Illegitimacy
- Impatience
- Inconsistency
- Lack of Identity
- Lack of Place
- Loss of Inheritance
- Nomad
- Restlessness
- Searching
- Unsettledness
- _____

PERFORMANCE
- Comparison
- Competition
- Coveting
- Driving
- Envy
- Jealousy
- People Pleasing
- Perfectionism
- Possessiveness
- Rivalry
- Striving
- Workaholism
- _____

REBELLION
- Confusion
- Contempt
- Deception
- Defiance
- Dishonor
- Disobedience
- Independence
- Insubordination
- Mistrust
- Resistance
- Self-Reliant
- Self-Sufficiency
- Self-Will
- Stubbornness
- Undermining
- Unsubmissiveness
- _____

REJECTION
- Expected Rejection
- Indirect Rejection
- Perceived Rejection
- Self-Rejection
- _____

A S

SHAME
- Anger
- Bad Boy/Girl
- Being Different
- Condemnation
- Disgrace
- Embarrassment
- Guilt
- Hatred
- Humiliation
- Illegitimacy
- Inferiority
- Regret
- Self-Accusation
- Self-Condemnation
- Self-Hate
- Self-Pity
- Sexual Sins
- _____
- _____
- _____
- _____

UNWORTHINESS
- Inadequacy
- Inferiority
- Insecurity
- Self-Accusation
- Self-Condemnation
- Self-Consciousness
- Self-Hate
- Self-Punishment
- Self-Sabotage
- _____
- _____

VICTIMIZATION
- Abandonment
- Betrayal
- Control
- Deportation
- Entrapped
- Helplessness
- Hopelessness
- Mistrust
- Passivity
- Predator
- Prejudice
- Self-Pity
- Slave Mentality
- Suspicion
- Trauma
- Unfaithfulness
- _____

GENERAL INDICATORS

A S

___ ___ **ADDICTIONS/ DEPENDENCIES**
___ ___ Alcohol
___ ___ Excessive Caffeine
___ ___ Cocaine
___ ___ Computers/Internet
___ ___ Downers/Uppers
___ ___ Food
___ ___ Gambling
___ ___ Marijuana
___ ___ Masturbation
___ ___ Nicotine
___ ___ Non-prescription Drugs
___ ___ Obsessive-Compulsive
___ ___ Overspending
___ ___ Pornography
___ ___ Prescription Drugs
___ ___ Sex
___ ___ Sleep Medication
___ ___ Sports
___ ___ Street Drugs
___ ___ Television
___ ___ Video Games
___ ___ _____
___ ___ _____
___ ___ _____

___ ___ **ANXIETY**
___ ___ Burden
___ ___ False Responsibility
___ ___ Fatigue
___ ___ Impatience
___ ___ Nervousness
___ ___ Panic Attacks
___ ___ Restlessness
___ ___ Stress
___ ___ Weariness
___ ___ Worry
___ ___ _____
___ ___ _____

___ ___ **BITTERNESS**
___ ___ Accusation
___ ___ Blaming
___ ___ Complaining
___ ___ Condemnation
___ ___ Criticalness
___ ___ Gossip
___ ___ Judging
___ ___ Murmuring
___ ___ Offended
___ ___ Ridicule
___ ___ Slander
___ ___ Unforgiveness
___ ___ _____

A S

___ ___ **DEATH**
___ ___ Abaddon (Rev. 9:11)
___ ___ Abortion
___ ___ Accidents
___ ___ Death Assignment
___ ___ Death Wish
___ ___ Death to Destiny
___ ___ Death Dreams
___ ___ Miscarriage
___ ___ Murder
___ ___ Premature Death
___ ___ Suicide
___ ___ Suicide Attempt
___ ___ Suicide Fantasies
___ ___ _____

___ ___ **DECEPTION**
___ ___ Blindness
___ ___ Cheating
___ ___ Confusion
___ ___ Denial
___ ___ Delusion
___ ___ Fraudulence
___ ___ Gender Identity Confusion
___ ___ Infidelity
___ ___ Justifying
___ ___ Lying
___ ___ Minimizing
___ ___ Naiveté
___ ___ Secretiveness
___ ___ Self-Deception
___ ___ Treachery
___ ___ Trickery
___ ___ Untrustworthiness
___ ___ _____

___ ___ **DEPRESSION**
___ ___ Dejection
___ ___ Discouragement
___ ___ Despair
___ ___ Despondency
___ ___ Gloominess
___ ___ Hopelessness
___ ___ Misery
___ ___ Oversleeping
___ ___ Sadness
___ ___ Self-Pity
___ ___ Suicide Attempt
___ ___ Suicide Fantasies
___ ___ Withdrawal
___ ___ _____

___ ___ **EMOTIONAL DEPENDENCY**
___ ___ Co-Dependency
___ ___ Enabling
___ ___ False Responsibility
___ ___ Parental Inversion
___ ___ _____

A S

___ ___ **ESCAPE**
___ ___ Apathy
___ ___ Avoidance
___ ___ Busyness
___ ___ Daydreaming
___ ___ Fantasy
___ ___ Forgetfulness
___ ___ Hiding
___ ___ Hopelessness
___ ___ Indifference
___ ___ Isolation
___ ___ Laziness
___ ___ Oversleeping
___ ___ Passivity
___ ___ Procrastination
___ ___ Suicide Fantasies
___ ___ Trance
___ ___ _____
___ ___ _____

___ ___ **FAILURE**
___ ___ Success/Failure Cycle
___ ___ Defeat
___ ___ Loss
___ ___ Performance
___ ___ Pressure to Succeed
___ ___ Striving
___ ___ Unfulfilled Destiny
___ ___ _____

___ ___ **FINANCIAL PROBLEMS**
___ ___ Bankruptcy
___ ___ Cheating
___ ___ Covetousness
___ ___ Debt
___ ___ Deception
___ ___ Delinquency
___ ___ Dishonesty
___ ___ Failure
___ ___ Fraud
___ ___ Greed
___ ___ Hoarding
___ ___ Idolatry of Possessions
___ ___ Illegitimate Gain
___ ___ Irresponsible Spending
___ ___ Job Failures
___ ___ Job Losses
___ ___ Lack
___ ___ Lost Inheritance
___ ___ Love of Money
___ ___ Neglect
___ ___ Poverty
___ ___ Robbing God (not tithing)
___ ___ Selfish Ambition
___ ___ Stealing
___ ___ Stinginess
___ ___ _____

A   S

___ ___ **GRIEF**
___ ___ Anguish
___ ___ Crying
___ ___ Despair
___ ___ Disappointment
___ ___ Heartbreak
___ ___ Hope Deferred
___ ___ Isolation
___ ___ Loss
___ ___ Pain
___ ___ Regret
___ ___ Sorrow
___ ___ Torment
___ ___ Weeping
___ ___ _____
___ ___ _____
___ ___ _____

___ ___ **IDENTITY ISSUES**
___ ___ Bisexual
___ ___ Confusion
___ ___ Effeminate Males
___ ___ Emos
___ ___ Gender Confusion
___ ___ Goth
___ ___ Homosexuality
___ ___ Lesbianism
___ ___ Loss of Self
___ ___ Masculine Females
___ ___ Self-Deception
___ ___ Self-Hate
___ ___ Transgender
___ ___ Transsexual
___ ___ Transvestite
___ ___ _____
___ ___ _____

___ ___ **MENTAL PROBLEMS**
___ ___ ADD/ADHD
___ ___ Alzheimer's Disease
___ ___ Bi-Polar Disorder
___ ___ Confusion
___ ___ Distraction
___ ___ Forgetfulness
___ ___ Hallucinations
___ ___ Hysteria
___ ___ Insanity
___ ___ Mind Binding
___ ___ Mind Blocking
___ ___ Mind Racing
___ ___ Obsessive-Compulsive
___ ___ Paranoia
___ ___ Schizophrenia
___ ___ Senility
___ ___ Stress Disorder
___ ___ _____

A   S

___ ___ **MOCKING**
___ ___ Blaspheming
___ ___ Cursing
___ ___ Cynical
___ ___ Laughing
___ ___ Profanity
___ ___ Ridicule
___ ___ Sarcasm
___ ___ Scorn
___ ___ Scoffing
___ ___ _____

___ ___ **NOT MOTIVATED**
___ ___ Irresponsibility
___ ___ Lack of Discipline
___ ___ Laziness
___ ___ Procrastination
___ ___ _____
___ ___ _____
___ ___ _____

___ ___ **PRIDE**
___ ___ Above Contradiction
___ ___ Arrogance
___ ___ Conceit
___ ___ Egotistical
___ ___ Haughtiness
___ ___ Leviathan
___ ___ Prejudice
___ ___ Self-Centeredness
___ ___ Self-Importance
___ ___ Self-Righteousness
___ ___ Superiority
___ ___ Suppression of Others
___ ___ Unteachable
___ ___ Vanity
___ ___ _____

___ ___ **RELIGION**
___ ___ Antichrist
___ ___ Betrayal
___ ___ Denominationalism
___ ___ Division
___ ___ Excessive Rules
___ ___ False Faith
___ ___ Hypocrisy
___ ___ Injustice
___ ___ Legalism
___ ___ New Age Practices
___ ___ Phariseeism
___ ___ Religiosity
___ ___ Religious Control
___ ___ Religious Performance
___ ___ Spiritual Pride
___ ___ Traditionalism
___ ___ Works Mentality
___ ___ _____
___ ___ _____

A   S

___ ___ **TRAUMA**
___ ___ Abuse, Emotional
___ ___ Abuse, Mental
___ ___ Abuse, Physical
___ ___ Abuse, Sexual
___ ___ Abuse, Spiritual
___ ___ Abuse, Verbal
___ ___ Accidents
___ ___ Divorce
___ ___ Imprisonment
___ ___ Loss
___ ___ Post Traumatic Stress Syndrome
___ ___ Rape
___ ___ Torture
___ ___ Violence
___ ___ War
___ ___ _____
___ ___ _____

___ ___ **UNBELIEF**
___ ___ Apprehension
___ ___ Cynicism
___ ___ Double Mindedness
___ ___ Doubt
___ ___ Fear of Being Wrong
___ ___ Intellectualism
___ ___ Mind Blocking
___ ___ Mistrust
___ ___ Rationalism
___ ___ Skepticism
___ ___ Suspicion
___ ___ Uncertainty
___ ___ _____

___ ___ **VIOLENCE**
___ ___ Abuse
___ ___ Arguing
___ ___ Bickering
___ ___ Cruelty
___ ___ Cursing
___ ___ Death
___ ___ Destruction
___ ___ Feuding
___ ___ Hate
___ ___ Militancy
___ ___ Murder/Abortion
___ ___ Retaliation
___ ___ Strife
___ ___ Torture/Mutilation
___ ___ War
___ ___ _____
___ ___ _____
___ ___ _____

OCCULT INDICATORS

A S

A S		A S		A S	
___ ___	**CONTROL**	___ ___	**FEAR**	___ ___	**INFIRMITIES/DISEASE**
___ ___	Anorexia	___ ___	Anxiety	___ ___	Allergies/Hay Fever
___ ___	Appeasement	___ ___	Bewilderment	___ ___	Arthritis
___ ___	Bulimia	___ ___	Burden	___ ___	Asthma
___ ___	Cutting	___ ___	Harassment	___ ___	Barrenness/Miscarriage
___ ___	Denial	___ ___	Heaviness	___ ___	Bone Problems
___ ___	Domineering	___ ___	Horror	___ ___	Cancer
___ ___	Double Binding	___ ___	Intimidation	___ ___	Circulatory Problems
___ ___	Enabling	___ ___	Over-Sensitivity	___ ___	Dementia
___ ___	False Responsibility	___ ___	Paranoia	___ ___	Diabetes
___ ___	Female Control	___ ___	Phobia	___ ___	Fatigue
___ ___	Jealousy	___ ___	Superstition	___ ___	Female Problems
___ ___	Manipulation	___ ___	Terror	___ ___	Heart Problems
___ ___	Male Control	___ ___	Timidity	___ ___	Joint Problems
___ ___	Occult Control	___ ___	Torment	___ ___	Lung Problems
___ ___	Passive Aggression	___ ___	Worry	___ ___	MS
___ ___	Passivity	___ ___	Fear of Authorities	___ ___	Migraines
___ ___	Possessiveness	___ ___	Fear of Being Abused	___ ___	Physical Abnormalities
___ ___	Pride (I know best)	___ ___	Fear of Being Alone	___ ___	Sinus Problems
___ ___	Selfishness	___ ___	Fear of Being Attacked	___ ___	Teeth/Gum Problems
___ ___	Scheming	___ ___	Fear of Being a Victim	___ ___	Viruses
___ ___	Through anger	___ ___	Fear of Being Wrong	___ ___	_____
___ ___	Through fear	___ ___	Fear of Conflict	___ ___	_____
___ ___	Through intimidation	___ ___	Fear of Death		
___ ___	Through silent treatments	___ ___	Fear of Demons	___ ___	**SEXUAL BONDAGE**
___ ___	Through threats	___ ___	Fear of Exposure	___ ___	Adultery
___ ___	Through withdrawal	___ ___	Fear of Failure	___ ___	Beastiality
___ ___	Witchcraft	___ ___	Fear of the Future	___ ___	Bisexuality
___ ___	_____	___ ___	Fear of Heart Attack	___ ___	Cybersex
___ ___	_____	___ ___	Fear of Inadequacy	___ ___	Defilement
___ ___	_____	___ ___	Fear of Infirmities	___ ___	Demonic Sex
___ ___	_____	___ ___	Fear of Intimacy	___ ___	Exposure
___ ___	_____	___ ___	Fear of Looking Stupid	___ ___	Fantasy Lust
		___ ___	Fear of Losing Control	___ ___	Fornication
		___ ___	Fear of Loss	___ ___	Frigidity
___ ___	**IDOLATRY OF**	___ ___	Fear of Man	___ ___	Homosexuality
___ ___	Appearance	___ ___	Fear of Marriage	___ ___	Illegitimacy
___ ___	Beauty	___ ___	Fear of Performing	___ ___	Incest
___ ___	Children	___ ___	Fear of Poverty	___ ___	Incubus
___ ___	Clothes	___ ___	Fear of Punishment	___ ___	Lesbianism
___ ___	Education	___ ___	Fear of Rejection	___ ___	Masochism
___ ___	Food	___ ___	Fear of Sexual Inadequacy	___ ___	Masturbation
___ ___	Intellectualism	___ ___	Fear of Submission	___ ___	Molestation
___ ___	Ministry	___ ___	Fear of Success	___ ___	Pedophile
___ ___	Money	___ ___	Fear of the Unknown	___ ___	Perversion
___ ___	Occupation	___ ___	Fear of Violence	___ ___	Pornography
___ ___	Position	___ ___	_____	___ ___	Premarital Sex
___ ___	Possessions	___ ___	_____	___ ___	Promiscuity
___ ___	Power	___ ___	_____	___ ___	Prostitution/Harlotry
___ ___	Social Status	___ ___	_____	___ ___	Rape
___ ___	Sports	___ ___	_____	___ ___	Sadism
___ ___	Spouse	___ ___	_____	___ ___	Seduction/Alluring
___ ___	Wealth	___ ___	_____	___ ___	Sexual Abuse
___ ___	_____	___ ___	_____	___ ___	Sodomy
___ ___	_____	___ ___	_____	___ ___	Succubus
___ ___	_____	___ ___	_____	___ ___	Uncleanness
				___ ___	Voyeurism
		___ ___	_____	___ ___	_____

A   S

OCCULT
___ ___ Abortion (Molech)
___ ___ Absalom Spirit
___ ___ Accident Proneness
___ ___ Ahab Spirit
___ ___ Animal Spirits
___ ___ Antichrist
___ ___ Astral Projection
___ ___ Astrology
___ ___ Automatic Writing
___ ___ Behemoth
___ ___ Black Magic
___ ___ Clairvoyance
___ ___ Conjuration
___ ___ Crystal Ball
___ ___ Death, Suicide
___ ___ Demon Worship
___ ___ Dispatching Demons
___ ___ Divination
___ ___ Eastern Meditation
___ ___ Eight Ball
___ ___ ESP
___ ___ Evil Eye
___ ___ False Gifts (Occult)
___ ___ Fortune Telling
___ ___ Freemasonry
___ ___ Hand Reading
___ ___ Handwriting Analysis
___ ___ Hexing
___ ___ Horoscopes
___ ___ Hypnosis
___ ___ I Ching
___ ___ Idolatry of _____
___ ___ Incantations
___ ___ Jezebel
___ ___ Leviathan
___ ___ Mediumship
___ ___ Mental Telepathy
___ ___ Necromancy
___ ___ Non-Christian Exorcism
___ ___ Occult Books
___ ___ Occult Control
___ ___ Occult Dedications
___ ___ Occult Victim
___ ___ Ouija Board
___ ___ Palm Reading
___ ___ Past Life Readings
___ ___ Pendulum Readings
___ ___ Psychic Healing
___ ___ Psychic Readings
___ ___ Python
___ ___ Reading Tea Leaves
___ ___ Reincarnation
___ ___ Satanic Worship
___ ___ Séances
___ ___ Sorcery
___ ___ Spells

A   S

___ ___ Spirit of Baccus (Mardi Gras)
___ ___ Spirit Guide(s)
___ ___ Spiritism
___ ___ Superstition
___ ___ Table Tipping
___ ___ Tarot Cards
___ ___ Third Eye
___ ___ TM
___ ___ Trance
___ ___ Vampire
___ ___ Voodoo
___ ___ Water Witching
___ ___ Werewolf
___ ___ White Magic
___ ___ Wicca
___ ___ Witchcraft
___ ___ _____

HAVE YOU EVER:

___ ___ Been involved in a 'Bloody Mary ritual'
___ ___ Cast a Spell or Hex
___ ___ Drank Blood or Urine
___ ___ Heard Violent Rap Music
___ ___ Had Masonic Jewelry
___ ___ Had Occult Jewelry
___ ___ Had Occult Books
___ ___ Had Witchcraft Books
___ ___ Had Pagan Fetishes
___ ___ Head Voices *(Please define)*
___ ___ Heard "Kill Yourself"
___ ___ Joined a Coven
___ ___ Played Dungeons & Dragons
___ ___ Made a Blood Pact
___ ___ Made a Blood Oath or Vow
___ ___ Participated in Martial Arts
___ ___ Seen a Sacrifice
___ ___ Seen Demons
___ ___ Seen Horror Movies
___ ___ Selected a Guru
___ ___ Used Mantras
___ ___ Visited Pagan Temples
___ ___ Visited Indian Burial Grounds
___ ___ _____

FAMILY INVOLVEMENT IN:

___ ___ Armstrong Radio Church
___ ___ Baha'i
___ ___ Buddhism
___ ___ Buffaloes
___ ___ Christadelphians
___ ___ Christian Education Society
___ ___ Christian Science
___ ___ College Fraternities
___ ___ College Sororities

A   S

___ ___ Daughters of Eastern Star
___ ___ Daughters of the Nile
___ ___ DeMolay Lodge
___ ___ Druids
___ ___ Eagles Lodge
___ ___ Eastern Religions
___ ___ Edgar Cayce
___ ___ Elks Lodge
___ ___ Foresters
___ ___ (The) Grange
___ ___ Hari Krishna
___ ___ Hinduism
___ ___ Indian Occult Rituals
___ ___ Inner Peace Movement
___ ___ Islam
___ ___ Jehovah's Witness
___ ___ Jobs Daughter's Lodge
___ ___ Kabbalah
___ ___ KKK
___ ___ Knights of Columbus
___ ___ Knights of Malta
___ ___ Knights of Pythias
___ ___ Knights of Templar
___ ___ Mardi Gras
___ ___ Masons
___ ___ Moonies
___ ___ Moose Lodge
___ ___ Mormonism
___ ___ Mystic Order of the Veiled Prophets of the Enchanted Realm
___ ___ New Age Movement
___ ___ Odd Fellows Lodge
___ ___ Orange Lodge
___ ___ Order of the Red Cross
___ ___ Rainbow Girls Lodge
___ ___ Rebekah's Lodge
___ ___ Reiki
___ ___ Religious Science
___ ___ Riders of the Red Robe
___ ___ Rosacrucianism
___ ___ Santeria
___ ___ Satanism
___ ___ Scientology
___ ___ Shamanism
___ ___ Shriners
___ ___ Silva Mind Control
___ ___ Spiritualism
___ ___ Swedenborgianism
___ ___ Theosophy
___ ___ Unitarian Church
___ ___ Voodoo
___ ___ The Way International
___ ___ White Shrine
___ ___ Witchcraft
___ ___ Woodmen of the World
___ ___ _____

Endnotes

1. The Grace Life Conference (Association of Exchanged Life Ministries, 1999),24.
2. Kylstra, Chester and Betsy, Ministry Tools, 3rd Edition (Hendersonville, NC, Restoring the Foundations Publishing, 2009) 32.
3. Egli, Jim, Encounter God Manual (Houston, TX, TOUCH Publications, 1999), 50.
4. Hunter, Joan, Joan Hunter Ministries, Pinehurst, TX. (taken from a conference teaching)
5. Strong, James, Strong's Exhaustive Concordance (1890).
6. cf Frost, Jack, Spiritual Slavery to Spiritual Sonship (Shippensburg, PA, Destiny Image Publishers, Inc., 2006) 39-44
7. Campbell, Ross, MD, How to Really Love Your Teenager (Colorado Springs, CO, Chariot Victor Publishing, 1981,1993) 73.
8. Thurman, Dr. Chris, The Lies We Believe (Nashville, TN, Thomas Nelson, Inc., 1989) 55-57.
9. Frangipane, Francis, The Three Battlegrounds (Cedar Rapids, IA, Arrow Publications, 1989) 48.
10. Kylstra, Chester and Betsy, Ministry Tools, 44.
11. ibid, page 43.
12. ibid, page 45.
13. ibid, page 45.
14. Kylstra, Chester and Betsy, Restoring the Foundations, My Story Application, www.rtfi.org, (2013), pages 10-11.
15. Kylstra, Chester and Betsy, Restoring the Foundations, 2nd Edition (Hendersonville, NC, Restoring the Foundations Publishing, 2001) 354.
16. Kylstra, Chester and Betsy, Shame-Fear-Control Stronghold Three CD Teaching Set (Hendersonville, NC, Restoring the Foundations Publishing, 1996-2011)
17. Kylstra, Chester and Betsy, Restoring the Foundations, 2nd Edition, 355.
18. Shiver, Jessica, Time of Singing (1989)
19. Bottari, Pablo, Encourager Church, Houston TX. (taken from a ministry training lecture)
20. Kylstra, Chester and Betsy, Restoring the Foundations, My Story Application, www.rtfi.org, (2013), pages 15-19.

www.ingramcontent.com/pod-product-compliance
Lightning Source LLC
Chambersburg PA
CBHW061929290426
44113CB00024B/2851